See Stormy Run

By Boyd Wright

Introduction by Susan Netboy

Founder of the Greyhound Protection League

authorHOUSE™

1663 LIBERTY DRIVE, SUITE 200
BLOOMINGTON, INDIANA 47403
(800) 839-8640
WWW.AUTHORHOUSE.COM

First published by AuthorHouse 10/18/04

ISBN: 1-4208-0419-7 (sc)

Library of Congress Control Number: 2004097579

Printed in the United States of America
Bloomington, Indiana

This book is printed on acid-free paper.

For Jean,

for Jamie, who raced into our lives,

and for all the valiant volunteers who rescue racing Greyhounds

Introduction

By Susan Netboy

Founder of the Greyhound Protection League

The plight of the racing Greyhound is a subject that has resonated throughout our society for over a decade. Whether the focus is the drama of the rescue effort, the sad fate of so many Greyhounds, or the dedication of the rescuers themselves – never before has a single breed of dog so captured the attention of the press and the heart of the American public. But it hasn't always been so. During his long service to mankind, the Greyhound has known both great benevolence and the depths of cruelty from the human beings who have guided his destiny.

Throughout his 5,000-year history as the premiere running dog, the Greyhound's unique athletic abilities have proven to be, at once, a curse and a blessing. As an esteemed coursing dog and companion in England, the breed once enjoyed the protection of nobility and laws that prohibited the killing of a Greyhound.

Sadly, all that would change as the centuries followed the inevitable course toward the supremacy of corporate greed and profit. The status of the Greyhound fell to a low ebb at the beginning of the 20th century when Greyhounds started chasing money around the oval track. With the advent of dog racing a new ethic guided the fate of the Greyhound: *win or die*. The Greyhound's long history as a gentle companion was ignored in order to justify the demise of the hundreds of thousands of Greyhounds who failed to make enough money to satisfy their owners. Neither the soft nuzzling of a condemned dog, nor the abject terror of others who waited deterred the executioner from his duties. Business was business – and the finish line dispensed no mercy.

Fortunately, the Greyhound's former reputation as a docile, loving companion could not be denied forever. After decades of being treated as nothing more than a disposable commodity, tens of thousands of retired racing Greyhounds have finally taken their rightful place as beloved pets in thousands of homes across America.

Anyone interested in learning more about adopting these wonderful dogs can call the Greyhound Protection League at 1-800-4HOUNDS or visit the league's web site at *greyhounds.org.*

Stormy, our book's hero, is one of the survivors. However, as the story unfolds we find that Stormy's path to true happiness and love is fraught with difficulty and gripping adventures. As he dodges the unsavory characters who threaten to destroy his life as a pet, Stormy is forced to rely on the same agility and speed that saved his life at the track. The reader is seized with fear as Stormy tries to solve his problems the only way he knows how: by running as fast as he can.

The author weaves a compelling story about the challenges that face the Greyhound rescue community as well as the dogs that volunteers work so diligently to save. As a veteran newspaperman, Boyd Wright brings immense insight into the human foibles and travails of his characters. His experiences as a life-long animal lover and adopter of his own rescued Greyhound lend great credibility to his intuitive view of animal psychology. The unique exploration of the bond that develops between a boy and his dog makes for a truly inspiring story that will captivate readers of any age.

See Stormy Run

Chapter One

I'm a racing Greyhound. When I was young, all I ever wanted to do was run. Run as hard and as long and as fast as I could. Run faster than all the other puppies in my litter. Run faster than any other dog in the world.

At least that's what I thought. Now I know better. I know there are more important things in life than running. But it took me a long time to learn that lesson. To let you understand what I'm talking about, I'll have to start at the beginning.

My name is Midnight Storm, and that's the name printed on all the racing forms in all the races that I ran. But you can call me

Stormy. Everybody does. I got my name because my father was Black Thunder and my mother was Lightning Lady. My father was a famous racer, but I never knew him. My mother raced, too, before her owners retired her for breeding. I don't know where she is now, but I loved her very much.

Looking back, my early life as a racer may sound exciting, but really it was dull. Even the running on the track is nothing but a blur in my mind now. All the tracks. They were all the same. When you're racing, for those few fleeting moments, your heart is beating, your feet are pounding, and every nerve in your body is stretched out hard and tight to think of nothing but speed, speed, speed. You don't focus on anything except what's ahead of you, and you want to get there first no matter who or what gets in your way.

That's my earliest real memory: running. Running with my littermates, my three brothers and four sisters. We would tear around our kennel yard chasing each other. Even then I tried to run faster than the others, and most of the time I did.

I also remember the day they took us into the office and each of us got our ears tattooed. Inside the left ear I got a special registered number for racing, and inside the right one numbers for my date of birth and place in the litter. Believe me, I was scared.

I can't remember much about our kennel keepers. We never saw them, except at feeding and exercise times. They seemed to change all the time, and I can't recall what they looked like, much less what their names were.

When I was a few months old, they turned us into a much bigger pen where we could really stretch our legs and run. And run and run. As always, I tried to be fastest. Then they put us into an even bigger run, and we ran with other young dogs our age, and I tried even harder.

Then we met our trainer, a big man with black boots and a big voice. He started by dragging lures like cans and bottles on a rope to get us to chase them. I didn't need those things. Then and later I never needed anything to follow. I never wanted to do anything but run and get to the finish line before anybody else.

The trainer wasn't mean, but he never seemed to notice us at all as individual puppies. He never petted us or even talked to us. Until one day, he took me by the collar and looked me over. "You're big and black and ornery," he said. "But you want to run, so we'll see what you can do."

With that he took me out every day onto the track with older dogs. Sometimes we would chase a whirligig, which is just a hunk of cloth on the end of a pole that keeps going around and around in a big circle. Sometimes he took us to run on a real oval track, and I liked that best of all.

That was when I really learned to run. I didn't care how I did it. I just had a fever to get there, so I did what came naturally. I churned up the track and never let anything stop me. If another dog got too close, I put my shoulder to him. I forged ahead and did what it takes to get to the end. I learned to cut in and out, to take the curves without slipping, to use my long tail to balance, and, above all, to keep my legs churning, churning, churning. I moved those legs so fast I let my body fly.

But I never tried to bite another dog just to get there first. I couldn't have even if I wanted to; we all wore muzzles, not only while racing but even while exercising.

I must have been about eighteen months old when the practicing was over and I ran my first real race. I remember the shouting of the crowd and the blur of the faces along the rail and all the way up into the grandstand. But the race wasn't much different from all the training heats we had run. I just ran as fast as I could, kept my balance on the turns, shouldered my way into that pack of eight dogs – and won.

The races went on like that, one after the other, usually for me about twice a week at so many different tracks I lost count. Sometimes we ran five-sixteenths of a mile, sometimes five-eighths, but it was all over in less than a minute. After all, we Greyhounds can cover the ground at about 40 miles an hour.

Always ahead of us was that lure. Silly people think it's a rabbit, but we dogs know better. It's just a phony object shaped like a rabbit that runs on a rail so we can chase it. I guess we do sort of follow it, but not really. Most of us would run whether that silly rabbit was there or not. We run because we want to, because that's what we're bred for, rabbit or no rabbit, real or phony.

I got better and better at getting out of the starting box on the fly, and I learned to run just as well from any of the eight positions, inside, outside and everywhere in between. Sometimes I won. Sometimes I finished second or third. Sometimes I slipped or got shoved aside and so came in way back in the pack. But I always ran my hardest. The dogs I ran against ran harder, too, and harder, and the competition kept getting harder.

Soon I got sent to different tracks in several different states. I never knew just where we were. I just know it took forever in the trucks to get there. To us dogs all the tracks looked the same. Just that lure up ahead, always just out of our reach, and the other dogs pounding alongside and the fans cheering, hoping their favorite would win and make them some money. I would like to think I made money for the nice people who bet on me, but we dogs never got to know anything about that.

But of course running was only part of my life. The rest of it was duller than you could ever imagine. I lived in a crate, a wire cage that measured only a few feet in each direction, barely room to turn around in. On the floor was just shredded newspaper; no toys, no chew things, nothing. The kennel keepers let us out three or four times a day to exercise. Even then we had our muzzles on. For a few minutes we could play, but we never had enough room to run properly. Then back we would go into the cages. The only other times we got out was to train or to race.

The food was far from tasty and there was never enough of it. Our owners wanted to keep us skinny and in fighting trim for the track.

When we moved around the country we always moved inside those cages. No real people ever talked to us, petted us or even paid attention to us. Boring, boring, boring.

And so the racing went on. I ran until I was five years old. Few dogs compete that long, but I guess my record was good enough for my owners to keep me going. I endured cuts and scrapes from skids on the track, cinders and dust in my eyes, even a nasty slash from the hind claws of a dog I was following. And I saw others suffer even more. We Greyhounds have powerful thigh muscles that drive us so hard they're all too apt to snap our long, skinny leg bones. If a bone breaks, that ends a dog's career and maybe his life.

I never had a chance to make good friends with my fellow racers. Too many tracks and too many changes. I did get friendly with a beautiful dark brindle named Fancy, who lived for a while in the cage stacked right above mine. Then one day, waiting for my race and watching hers, I saw her slip on the outside curve of a muddy track, slam into the fence and lie still. When they picked her up, one poor hind leg stuck out at an ugly angle. They carried her away and I never saw her again.

Those years of racing seem like a dream now, a fuzzy dream and not too pleasant. A few moments of wild exertion, then the bitterness of defeat or the brief joy of victory. Over too soon, then back to the cage. Back to captivity and loneliness.

For a long time I thought this was what life was all about. Remember, I didn't know any other kind of life. Just living in a crate and running. Putting all my strength into a race that lasted less than a minute. All over in a flash, and for what? For winning, I suppose. But was that enough?

I began to see that running and winning really were not enough. But I didn't know what else there could be. Slowly there grew in me a great ache. I didn't know what it was. I couldn't have described it. But I know now. What I wanted without knowing it was to love and be loved.

Chapter Two

My racing career ended all of a sudden. I was five years old, close to the limit in age but still running strong. In fact I won my last race, and I can still hear the cheering. But the next day I found myself in my crate back in the truck and the day after that in a vet's office getting all kinds of treatment, some of it nasty but probably good for me. The day after that a van rolled up to our holding area and five of us were loaded aboard. It was the first time I had ever traveled outside my crate.

The van was driven by a friendly, motherly woman whom I later learned to know as my Rescue Lady. One by one she dropped each of us off at a different house.

I entered my first private home! Believe me, it was an experience. I didn't know a kitchen from a bedroom. It was scary. I had to learn about carpets and sofas and muddy feet and how to climb stairs. The woman who lived in the house treated me all right, but she was too busy to give me much attention. She had two Greyhounds of her own.

Those live-in Greyhounds were far from friendly. They made me to understand that I was just a temporary visitor. For me, they explained, this was only a foster home. I asked one of them, an elderly gray-bearded Greyhound, what would happen to me. He shook his head. "I don't know," he said. "The rescue people are trying to get you adopted."

"What does that mean?" I asked.

The graybeard sniffed. "You have a lot to learn. It means the rescue people are trying to find you a home, a real home where you can stay put."

"Do you think they can?" I asked anxiously.

"Sometimes they can do it, sometimes not. It depends on you. If the people who come to look at you like you enough, they'll take you home. If they don't like you, they won't."

"Then what happens?" I was getting worried.

The graybeard just shrugged.

I wasn't encouraged when I heard my Rescue Lady, just before she went back to her van, tell the foster-home lady, "Stormy is so big, I'm afraid we're going to have a problem. So many people don't want a big dog."

I felt even worse when the foster lady answered, "And he's black. For some reason people are prejudiced against black dogs. Maybe black dogs look threatening."

At that moment I vowed never to act threatening but always be friendly even when I didn't feel like it.

The next few weeks at my foster home were a little more pleasant than living in a cage at the track, but not much. Those resident Greyhounds made me uncomfortable. I certainly had not found love, whatever that was. And I fretted about my future.

A few people came to see if they wanted to adopt me, but they never stayed long. One day I heard the foster-home lady talking to my Rescue Lady on the telephone. "This dog, Stormy, is five years old, you know," she said. "Everybody wants a younger dog. I wish you had given me a two or three-year-old. I don't know if we'll ever place him."

My spirits sagged to a new low. Days passed. The foster lady paid even less attention to me now. She played with her other Greyhounds and took them for walks, but me she ignored. She even seemed to give me my twice-a-day feeding grudgingly. After a while nobody came to look at me at all.

One day my Rescue Lady came to the door and I was put back into her van. The foster lady's last words were, "Sorry, I just couldn't keep him any longer. Good luck."

The Rescue Lady said, "Thanks for trying," and drove me a long way to another house. Here I found a new foster lady and a foster man, her husband. Again, they didn't pay much attention to me. After all, what could I expect? They were just people willing to keep me for a short while in the hope of finding somebody who would adopt me, who really wanted me. I knew this now and, believe me, it made me uneasy. I felt like living on borrowed time. And I guess that's really just what I was doing.

This new house also had a live-in Greyhound in residence. A big red brindle named Rex. The dogs at the other home had seemed standoffish, but this dog acted downright mean. He didn't like me being on his territory. For the first day we ignored each other. The next day my new foster lady put our bowls of food at opposite ends of the kitchen and left us alone. I had just started to eat when Rex leaped across the room, shouldered me aside and started to gobble my food. What was I supposed to do?

I growled. Then I snarled. Rex kept eating. At that I tore into him. We went at it hot and heavy, rolling around that kitchen trying to bite and claw. I heard the lady scream. Then the man came at us with a broom and broke up the fight.

Neither Rex nor I had hurt each other except for a scratch or two. I was hustled out onto the back porch and stayed there most of the day. In the late afternoon my Rescue Lady came in that same van that had taken me to other places and I was bundled in again. This time she took me to her own house. On the way she didn't say much, just pursed her lips and shook her head. I could see that I had become a problem.

The trouble was that my poor Rescue Lady was finding it hard to line up even a foster home, let alone a permanent place, for me. But, bless her heart, she certainly tried. She was one of the kindest and hardest working people I've known. An elderly, gentle lady, she dressed always in dog-comfortable clothes. I loved to sniff her because she smelled so deliciously of pure essence of Greyhound. Her whole life was dogs, and I thank my lucky stars that I had her for a guardian angel.

After a few days she drove me to still another house. We were met by a mother and father and a little boy. My Rescue Lady told them, "Stormy got in a fight at the last home, but he's really very friendly. I think he'll be good with your son if you give him a chance."

This time I really wanted to make a go of it. And it wasn't hard at all. The house was different from the others I had known. It stood on a quiet street with a fenced-in backyard with plenty of bright sunlight and fine shade trees. Inside I had a comfortable bed in the kitchen and another one in the family room. The mother and father were kind to me and made me feel at home.

But it was Davy, their little boy, who made all the difference. He and I hit it off right away. Davy asked if his folks would buy still another bed for me in his bedroom. They did and I slept by his side every night. As soon as he got home from school, he would snap on my leash and we would go for long walks together.

I think the happiest day of my life was when Davy's father announced at the dinner table one evening, "Well, I got the adoption papers back for Stormy today. We've adopted him, and he's legally ours."

"Wow!" Davy shouted. "You mean Stormy's really ours and nobody can take him away from us?"

"That's right, son."

Davy got up from the table and gave his father a big kiss. Then he kissed his mother. I felt like kissing them, too, so I gave each a lick and they made a big fuss over me. Then Davy threw his arms around my neck.

Later I heard Davy's mother tell his father, "Thank you, John, for adopting the dog. I've never seen Davy look so happy."

Davy's father said, "I hope it will be good for both of them."

As for me, I couldn't have been happier. This was what I had missed all my life. A family that really wanted me. A home, yes, but more. Much more. Love.

Chapter Three

My new life seemed almost too good to be true. Spring passed and summer and Davy and I spent whole days together. I was so happy that I didn't realize something could be missing in Davy's life. I sensed that although we had each other for company, he was lonely. He never played much with other children. I even noticed a kind of barrier between him and his mother and father. Not that they weren't good parents. They really were. They took good care of Davy just as they did of me. But somehow I felt a stangeness I couldn't put my paw on.

There was one thing I did notice, although I didn't give it much thought at the time. In my own family my brothers and sisters are all different colors — black, fawn, red, brindle and even gray (although Greyhound breeders call that particular color blue). So dogs take skin and coat colors for granted, but I don't think some humans have learned to do that yet. Anyway, I did notice that Davy's parents were white but that he, just like me, was black.

Then one day I learned how this came to be. On our walks Davy would often take me to a park with a pleasant hill that overlooked the suburbs all around us. That summer we spent many afternoons there. He would sit stroking my head and back and I would lie there looking up into his face. We talked. Of course, I didn't really talk. Dogs can't. At least not with humans. But we can listen and we can understand. So in a way Davy and I really did talk together.

One day Davy said, "Stormy, I think I know why you and I get along so well. You're adopted and so am I. My parents adopted you, and they adopted me, too. I didn't even realize I was adopted until I started growing up."

Davy was quiet for a minute, then he said, "I can see why it's tough for you. It's been kinda tough for me, too. It's not always easy when people see you don't even look like your parents."

I licked his hand.

"I don't even know who my real parents are," he went on. "I'm not sure I really want to know, but I guess I'm kinda curious. I love my parents — I mean my Mom and Dad here. I wouldn't want to hurt

18

them by going to look for my other parents. But still . . . Maybe I'll just have to figure it all out when I get older. Do you understand?"

I licked him again just to show I did understand.

I don't know if I can explain it, but the fact that Davy and I were both adopted, that life had aimed us down the same path, made me feel wonderfully comforted. Right away it seemed to strengthen the bond between us. I had loved him before; now I loved him more than ever. And I think maybe he loved me more, too.

Funny thing about life. Just when things start going well, wham! Something comes along to knock your whole world out of kilter. So with me. I had been trying so long to find a real home, to find somebody to adopt me. Now my dream had come true. And with it I had found the wonderful joy of loving and being loved by the one human who meant more to me than anything else in the world.

As I say, I had all this, and then suddenly everything got snatched away. I was out in the backyard nosing around, doing nothing in particular, when I heard my beloved Davy crying. Naturally I dashed back to get let into the house. Davy and his parents were sitting at the kitchen table. It was a family conference and it looked grim. Davy sprang up and threw his arms around me, sobbing.

"We have to move," he wailed. "And they won't let me take you!"

"Davy, Davy," his father said. "I know it's hard. I have to take this job. You'll understand when you get older. We have to go overseas. They don't allow us to take dogs because of quarantines. When we get settled there maybe we can get another dog. Meanwhile, we'll find a good home for Stormy, I promise."

My world crumbled. How could I live without my Davy? And that "good home" promise chilled me, too. After all the efforts the Rescue Lady had made to place me, it was going to have to start all over again.

I won't tell you of the dreadful sadness of those last couple of weeks before Davy and his family left. Davy cried most of the time, and, believe me, I cried, too. On the last day before the move, the Rescue Lady came back for me. She was nice about it. "Not your fault this time, Stormy," she said. "Now we'll just have to see what we can do."

That Rescue Lady really knew dogs. Right from the start, when she had first taken me and the others from the track, she tried mightily to put me into the best temporary foster home possible, and then she kept trying hard to find me a permanent home. And, as I was to learn much later, the good folks who kept the foster homes always tried hard, too. These dedicated people poured unselfish effort and love into caring for Greyhounds until permanent homes could be found. The trouble was that in my case, no matter how hard anybody tried, things never seemed to work out.

My Rescue Lady, bless her, never made a fuss over me. She took good care of me, but she didn't pet me much or even talk to me. Now I know why.

To start with, she was always busy. She had plenty of other dogs to take from place to place, to try to find even temporary foster homes, never mind the endless search for permanent adoption homes. She just didn't have a chance to get close to one particular dog. But, more than that, I think she was wise enough to know that she shouldn't love any one of us too much. We rescued dogs lived a tough life getting shuttled from home to home. This kind lady knew that separations were hard enough and she didn't want us to get hurt even more when we had to leave her.

So she tried hard to place us, but she also kept us just a bit at arm's length. I wasn't wise enough to understand that then, but now I know better and I honor her for it.

A few days later the Rescue Lady put me in her van, and this time she wore a big smile. "I think you'll like where I'm taking you, Stormy," she said. "But please do try to be good. Don't blow it!"

But would you believe it? I did manage to blow it. Here's how:

We drove a long way, well out of the suburbs and into the country. We turned off the main road to take a dirt track back into the woods and up a hill, stopping finally at a pleasant cottage built to look like a log cabin. This was to be my new home.

21

An elderly man and his elderly wife greeted us at the door. Right away I liked them, and as the days passed I liked them better and better. They were quiet and, I guess, kind of lonely out there in the country. Anyway, they made much of me, but life wasn't very exciting. My Rescue Lady had impressed on them that like all Greyhounds I loved to run so they should be careful to take me out only on a leash. The trouble was these nice folks were so old that they never took me far, and I always felt the need for more exercise. I longed to run. And run and run.

Still, life was pleasant enough. The old couple never came close to taking the place of Davy in my heart, but I really liked them and I would have been content to live with them.

But it was not to be. The old folks seldom left the house. About once a week one or the other would take their battered car to go shopping while the other stayed with me. Then one afternoon, the old man told me they were both going out. "You'll be all alone, Stormy," he said. "We trust you to be a good boy, and we'll be back before you know it."

He really was kind. The old lady patted me, too. The last thing she said was, "Take care of the house for us, Stormy."

They drove away and I snoozed on my bed in the kitchen. Suddenly I awoke to a terrible crash, and the cabin's back door burst open. A giant black bear stood in the doorway on his hind legs and roared at me. Then he dropped to all fours and ambled into the kitchen, snout to floor, snuffling and grunting.

What was I supposed to do? I'm a dog and I'm supposed to be a watchdog, after all. I was in charge of the home. I saw my duty. Without even thinking about it, I charged at that bear, growling as fiercely as I could. Never mind that he outweighed me at least six to one. I tore at him, darting back and forth to stay away from those terrible paws with their terrible claws. The bear roared and swiped at me, but I managed to stay just out of reach. We both whirled around and around, me keeping to the outside of the frantic circle and my opponent always turning to meet me head on.

I know that bear had come in looking for food. But now he found more trouble than he had bargained for. I think in another minute or two he could have backed me into a corner and done for me. But I was nimble, and after a while the great beast just gave up. With a disgusted snort he turned tail and waddled back out the door and off into the woods.

I felt good. I had hardly a scratch on me, and I had managed to rout a dreadfully dangerous enemy and save the home of my adoptive parents. Of course, that neat kitchen had become a total mess, the table overturned, pots, pans, dishes, cans, everything scattered about the floor, the linoleum ripped, the door gone, deep scratches everywhere.

When the car drove up, I rushed to meet my folks, tail wagging, expecting well-deserved praise. All was fine until they got into the kitchen. Then I thought the pair of them were going to throw a fit. I might have known. They had no way of realizing that a bear had been there, and I had no way of telling them. They just assumed all that damage was my doing. The first thing they did was get on the phone to my Rescue Lady to tell her they couldn't keep me. She took me away that very evening and I never saw that old couple again.

Of course the Rescue Lady thought this was all my fault, too. I thank my stars for her wonderfully forgiving heart. Her patience with me knew no bounds. All she said was, "Well, Stormy, we're just going to have to try again."

Chapter Four

This time I stayed several days with the Rescue Lady and a handful of other Greyhounds waiting for homes. Then one afternoon she announced, "Maybe this will work for you, Stormy. We'll see."

I noticed that she didn't sound nearly as cheerful about my prospects as she used to. And I couldn't blame her. I knew I was challenging her to become perhaps the hardest dog she had ever tried to place.

On the way over she said something I've never forgotten. "Stormy," she declared, "you're such a loving dog, I'll find a home for you if it's the last thing I ever do."

She took me to a small house in the suburbs. My new mistress was Amy, a young woman just out of college. She lived alone, and from my rescuer's point of view the best thing for me was that Amy worked at home.

"Oh, he'll never be by himself, so he won't be able to get into any trouble," Amy assured the Rescue Lady. "I'll take him everywhere with me."

If my patient Rescue Lady had any doubts, she didn't show it. I must say she was a real optimist.

Amy and I hit it off well. She was sweet and kind to me. If she had a fault, she was too sweet. She smothered me with kisses. That's fine, as far as it goes. Any dog loves to be loved. But Amy did overdo it at times. I loved her, too, I guess, but to tell the truth, it was hard for me truly to love any human being with all my heart. I had given that heart of mine to Davy. Nobody could take his place. Maybe that sounds unfair and maybe I should have been more grateful to Amy, but that's just how it was.

When Amy was through working at her computer for the day she would take me on long walks. Sometimes she would put me in her car and we would go out into the country. I liked those rambles best.

One late afternoon we crossed a pleasant field just as shadows from the neighboring woods were closing in on us. As always, Amy had me on my leash. Suddenly, right under my feet, a rabbit bounded up and raced for the trees. I guess I acted the way most Greyhounds would. I forgot everything except that rabbit, and I jerked the leash out of Amy's hand. Into the woods I tore right on the heels of the rabbit. He darted and twisted and turned, trying his best to lose me.

On and on we chased. I lost all track of time and of distance. I didn't even hear Amy, although she must have been calling frantically after me.

Finally the rabbit plunged into a bramble thicket and I realized I could never get him out of there. I skidded to a stop. And then I remembered Amy. I had no idea where she was or where I was. It was getting dark, and everything was deathly quiet.

The chase had taken me out of the woods and away from the fields to an overgrown empty lot on the edge of town. Garbage and abandoned tires lay next to the bramble patch. As I tried to work out my bearings I heard a strange noise. It took me a moment to realize what it was. Then it came to me. It was the faint wail of a child. Listening and sniffing, I circled the desolate dump area. Then I found the source of the sound. Behind a clump of bushes lay a little girl curled almost into a ball and crying, crying, crying as if her heart would break.

I sniffed at her and tried to reach her face and lick it. She sat up and the bawling stopped. In another moment she threw her arms around my neck. Then the sobbing started again.

I had trouble understanding her baby voice, but she kept saying something like, "Oh, doggie, doggie, I'm so glad you found me. I'm lost, but it's all right now."

I was in a dither. How could I tell her I was lost, too? We made a fine pair.

So I just tried to comfort that little girl as best I could. By now it was completely dark. Pretty soon, with me licking her and she gradually getting a little calmer, I was able to think. Then it came to me. I did the best thing I could think of. I stood back from her a little, lifted my muzzle and barked. I didn't just bark, I howled, too. I howled long and hard. I think the whole country must have heard me.

It seemed a long time, but it probably took only a few minutes. Somebody must have called the police, because a squad car with lights flashing and sirens blaring bore down on us. Two cops jumped out. One picked up the little girl and the other took hold of the leash I was still dragging.

After that everything happened in a hurry. More police cars arrived and even an ambulance. Then came a whole host of people on foot who must have been out searching the area for the lost child.

They even brought a bloodhound with them, and he and I touched noses. I could tell he was a real professional and it made me feel good when he told me, "Well done!"

Then the little girl's parents arrived. The mother threw her arms around me and called me a hero. I just tried to look modest.

Then Amy got there. She hugged me, too, and cried. After that a truck carrying a whole team of TV people arrived. They took pictures of all of us. I really felt like the Dog of the Year.

When we got home Amy made me look at the TV. "There," she told me, "you're famous. You saved a life! They should give you a medal."

I went over and sniffed the television set. I had done it before, and, believe me, there's nothing there. If it were real it would have a smell and it doesn't. Humans are silly to sit watching it all the time.

Being a hero didn't change my life much. People forget things in a hurry. Life with Amy was pleasant. Not exciting, you understand, but pleasant. I began to think that maybe, after everything, I had found a real home.

But it wasn't to be. Shawn was the trouble. He was stocky with muscles he liked to show off and tattoos on his arms, and he rode a motorcycle. And he wanted Amy.

Shawn started dropping by the house every few days. Soon he came every day. Often he took Amy out and I was left alone. I wasn't jealous. Not really. In fact, I enjoyed a little peace and quiet by myself. But then Shawn started hanging around the house all the time. And he started looking at me as if I was in the way. I didn't like that much, but I figured that if he made Amy happy, that was all right.

But he didn't make Amy happy. Not all the time anyway. At first she just seemed to like him, then I think she fell in love with him. But he took advantage of her. A dog can tell. He began ordering her around, making her do things she didn't want to do. He became more and more bossy, and I could see Amy was getting more and more unhappy. They argued a lot, but he always shouted louder than she did. One day she didn't do something Shawn wanted her to do quickly enough and he hauled off and smacked her hard across the face.

What was I supposed to do? I couldn't let him get away with that. I snarled and bared my teeth. I didn't mean to hurt him, just give him a good warning. But then he closed his fist and swatted me right on the muzzle.

At that I saw red. I snapped at the hand that hit me. He hollered bloody murder and started to kick me. Amy screamed and rushed between us. Shawn shoved her aside so hard that she fell to the floor. Then Shawn grabbed one of the kitchen chairs and came at me.

That did it. I dodged under the chair and lunged upwards. This time I clamped my jaws onto his forearm. I don't think I chomped too hard, but it was enough for him to scream a string of ugly words and bolt from the room, slamming the door.

Amy flung her arms around me sobbing. Her mouth was bleeding where the brute had socked her.

Through the door Shawn yelled, "You keep that mutt right there! Do you hear me? He's a vicious killer! I'm calling the cops to get him shot!"

Then I heard him shouting to the police on his cell phone. Now I knew I was in big trouble. Real life-and-death trouble this time. I hated to leave Amy, but there was nothing else for it. The kitchen window stood open to the June breeze. I made a leap, springing from my hind legs with enough force to crash right through the screen. I hit the ground running and never looked back.

I ran and ran and ran. Well, I had always wanted to run, hadn't I? And ever since I had left the track, I had never been able to run enough. So now I just let it all out. I ran and kept running, down streets, across intersections, through backyards, leaping fences, dodging traffic, until my sides heaved, my heart pounded and the pads of my feet felt sore as boils.

Finally, I stopped to drink thirstily from a muddy puddle and to take stock of my situation. It wasn't good. I had lost another home, and this time I couldn't count on my kind, patient Rescue Lady to find me a new one.

Chapter Five

All the rest of that day I wandered aimlessly down those tree-shaded suburban streets. I stared forlornly at the fronts of the neat houses, knowing that family life and perhaps real companionship and love lived behind those walls. More than ever I wished, oh how I wished, that I could find a lasting home of my own.

I spent most of the night curled under bushes at the edge of a small park. The next morning I started wandering again. Drivers slowed their cars to stare at me, then moved on. Twice I spotted police cars, and I gave them a wide berth.

And now I was hungry. About midday I heard the cheerful shouting of children, and, following the sounds, I came to a schoolyard. Kids by the dozen were sprawled on the ground or seated at long tables eating lunch. The food smelled so good I could hardly stand it.

I went up to one of the tables, tale wagging politely.

"Look at the cute doggie!" one girl squealed, and she gave me a piece of her sandwich.

"He's so skinny," another girl cried. "No wonder he's hungry." She gave me a whole sugar donut. After that the other kids began to compete to see who could give me the most to eat. I felt like a rock star.

"This is a cool dog," one boy said. "I wonder who he belongs to." He took hold of my collar and tried to read the tags, but I was having none of that. I backed away politely and accepted a slab of cake from a kid at the next table.

I think those generous children would have gone on feeding me until I burst if a janitor hadn't come out of the schoolhouse with a furious frown on his face. "Lay off that," he told the children. "We don't want no dog making a mess here."

He, too, made a grab for my collar, but I sidestepped him. Right off I disliked the man. Small and scrunched up with a mouth that puckered, he was one of those people who seem so unhappy and angry at the world that they want everybody else to feel the same way.

He made another grab at me and I dodged again. Now he looked so sore I knew that if he ever did get me, I'd be in trouble.

Then a lady came out of the schoolhouse. She was young and pretty, but she acted with authority and right away the kids stopped fooling around. She must have been the principal because even after the school bell rang she kept on talking.

She held out her hand palm down to let me smell her knuckles, so I knew she had to be a dog person. I had no worries about letting her read my tags.

"Children," the principal told the kids, "this dog was an honest-to-goodness racing Greyhound. After he finished his days at the track he was saved by a rescue organization and placed in a home for adoption."

You could tell the kids were interested. The principal held the attention of everybody except the surly janitor. He stood there mumbling to himself.

"Do you know what happens to most Greyhounds when they are too old to race?" the principal asked.

Even though we were outdoors, the children treated her with real respect. Some put their hands up.

"The dogs get killed," one kid volunteered.

"That's right," the principal said. "They get euthanized. That means put to death. And can you guess how many of these poor dogs are destroyed right at the prime of their lives if homes can't be found for them?"

Nobody answered.

"Many thousands," the lady said sadly. "A few thousand do get placed for adoption, but many, many more beautiful dogs, splendid racing animals who have earned a good life after the track, are just put down." She tightened her hand on my collar, and I could tell she felt thankful I had escaped this fate.

"Now," she said, "time to get back to class. I'll just call the number on this dog's collar to make sure he gets back to his owners. Meanwhile, Mr. Jensen can take care of him."

She handed me over to that beady-eyed janitor, and suddenly I didn't feel happy at all. After the others had gone inside, he tightened his hold on my collar and hustled me around the side of the school and shoved me into a little closet that smelled of cleaning fluid and dirty mops. "That'll keep you for a while," he muttered.

That dank, dark miserable prison of a closet proved to be one of the nastiest places I've ever been held in. I couldn't settle down. Sure I was worried, but I started to feel another problem coming on. The air in there made it hard to breathe, yet that wasn't the worst part. Those good kids had fed me so much food so fast that my stomach started to rebel. I felt queasy. Then I felt queasier and queasier. Pretty soon I brought up a good part of my hasty lunch, and you can bet that made the atmosphere in the closet even tougher to take.

An hour later the janitor opened the door. When the smell and the sight of my mess hit him, he gasped and swore. In fact the aroma hit him so hard, he took a step backward. That gave me just room to push past him out into the sunlight and the clean air and freedom.

I didn't bother to run too fast. Out in the open I knew that if I didn't want him to, he could never lay a hand on me. I loped downhill away from the school and met a bunch of boys headed the same way and bound for their afternoon athletics. They made a fuss over me and whistled and called, but I was nervous enough now to keep anybody from touching me. Still they were friendly and I hung around with them until we reached a big athletic field. A fence enclosed an oval track — a beautiful oval track much like the ones I had raced on for so many years.

I marveled at that track, and I started to relive all the old memories. I hadn't enjoyed a run around a real track for months. Suddenly I ached with all my being to sprint on a nice level, beautifully groomed oval just one more time.

The temptation was too much. When the boys entered the gate, I sidled through with them and started to run. They cheered and thought it splendid fun. Several even tried to run with me, but of course I left them far behind. Around and around I ran. I can hardly tell you how great it felt. We Greyhounds are born to run. Sometimes we just have to let go and let our legs do what comes naturally.

I ran and ran and ran, gulping in the delicious air. I felt my legs limber up. They stretched and hardened and gradually found the motion and the rhythm they were made for. I hit my stride then and poured it on. The boys yelled just the way track fans used to in the old days. That made me run faster and faster.

When I had run my full, I stopped, panting luxuriously. I enjoyed that glorious tingly feeling that comes after a good romp. Then I darted back to the admiring boys. I'm afraid I let my guard down. They wanted so badly to pet me that I let them.

Then abruptly the gate to the track clanged, and Jensen, the janitor, stalked in. "Hold onto that dog," he ordered. "Don't let him go."

Before I knew it, the man had his hand on my collar, and, despite protests from my young admirers, he marched me out of the track back to school. This time there would be no escape. He shoved me into the back of a greasy, ill-smelling van and went around to the driver's door.

Just then the principal came out and handed the janitor a slip of paper. "I've been on the phone to the Greyhound rescue people," she said. "Here's the address for you to take him to."

She reached through the window and patted my head. "Be a good boy," she told me. "I'm sure they'll get you back to your adopted home."

Jensen gunned the motor. On the way out of the school grounds he turned back to me. "Adopted home is it? I've got a better idea. Any dog that can run like you has gotta be worth money. We'll see what we can do."

I saw greed written all over his face, and I didn't like the look of it one little bit.

Chapter Six

My worst fears were realized. That ugly janitor wasn't about to take me back to my Rescue Lady. Instead he drove me to his own home nearby, a rundown house with a front yard filled with a dead auto and rotting piles of junk. He shoved me into the backyard, which was even filthier. Here I found three other dogs all kept prisoners by a sturdy wire fence.

My companions in captivity proved civil enough, but to a dog they lacked spirit. No wonder. They told me they were fed only when Jensen or his wife happened to think of it, and even then they got only a meager ration of slops.

The smallest of my fellow captives, a beautiful little white Bichon Frise, proved a bit more hopeful than the others. "I have a mistress who loves me very dearly," she told me. "This awful man, Jensen, kidnapped me, and I think he's holding me until my owner pays a ransom."

"That's right," chimed in an older dog, a part-Beagle. "She's a dog-show champion and worth a lot of money. Jensen hopes to make a big profit off her."

"It's not just that I'm a champion," returned the Bichon. "It's that my mistress loves me so very much. I'm sure she'll pay anything to get me back."

I looked at the other two dogs, the Beagle mix and a shaggy fellow who appeared to be mostly Shepherd. They didn't look like show dogs, but I was too polite to say so.

The Shepherd saved me embarrassment by explaining, but what he said was hardly encouraging. "I'm certainly not a valuable dog," he admitted. "So I have a deadly fear that this man, Jensen, wants to sell us to the vivisectionists."

"Who are they?" I asked.

"They're people who cut dogs up for experiments."

"You can't mean it," I said.

The part-Beagle spoke up. "He means this guy makes money by selling dogs to clinics where they perform medical research." Then he added darkly, "Only the lucky ones get killed outright. Most of the others get tortured with drugs and knives and all sorts of horrible surgery."

I couldn't believe it, but the other dogs nodded. "We've seen the truck that came for some of our friends," they assured me.

My mind boggled. How could any human being, even this mean janitor, be so evil? You see, I still had a lot to learn about the ways of the world. I know better now. I've learned that humans can be wonderfully kind and generous – in fact, just like dogs – but also that some human creatures are depraved enough to do anything for money.

My companions seemed so helpless that I felt I had to cheer them up. "Let's see if there isn't a way out of here," I suggested.

"No good," said the Beagle. "We've all tried."

"Well, let's try some more," I urged as optimistically as I could. I led them on a tour of our backyard prison. They were right. That fence was plenty tight. The bottom was even buried right into the ground. There was no way to dig out. And the wire was stretched so high that even I couldn't jump it.

I figured and figured, but there didn't seem any way to escape from that stockade. Obviously Jensen was an old hand at holding and mistreating dogs. So I started to concentrate on Mrs. Jensen. We didn't see her much, but some mornings while her husband was at work she came out of the back door with a pail of slops, our meal for the day. She would ladle this mess into four rusty, dirt-encrusted dishes, then retreat into the house.

I would love to take credit for how I tricked her, but I shouldn't. I didn't think things out as much as just follow my instinct. Since there seemed no other way, I simply did what a Greyhound does best. I ran.

I waited until the old lady came out with the slops. She wasn't much to look at, big and raw-boned, almost a head taller than her measly husband. Like him, she always seemed angry. She looked tough, and I decided to find out just how tough she really was.

As soon as she came out, I started to run. It wasn't easy. That fenced-in backyard wasn't much bigger than a good-sized room, and piles of junk lay everywhere.

Now a Greyhound loves to have plenty of space to run, but if we have to, we can run in small places, too. I'm lucky to have a long tail, black like the rest of me with a shiny white tip at the end. I'm proud of this tail. But, more important, it served me well in racing and it served me well now. I use it as a rudder. It streams straight out behind me. When I take a sharp turn, my tail maintains my balance, keeps me upright and moving fast.

Of course, running on a nice level oval track is one thing. The curves aren't that sharp. Running around that handkerchief-size yard was something else. But now I stretched my tail out behind me, reached out ahead with my nose, and let my feet tear me round and round. Once or twice I skidded, but mostly, thanks to that trusty rudder-tail, I kept my footing.

My target was Mrs. Jensen. At first I started whirling around the far side of the yard closest to the fence, but then I made my circles tighter and tighter. I closed in on the lady as she stood there, mouth agape. When I got almost close enough to touch her, she really got scared. She must have thought I would crash into her at my almost 40 miles an hour. She hollered then, dropped her pail of slop and even picked up a length of two-by-four lying on one of those messy piles.

She raised that block of wood to strike me, but I was too quick for her. On the next zip around I circled close enough to send the two-by-four flying from her hand. All the while I was nudging her away from the house toward the back gate. One more go around and I whizzed by so close I almost knocked her over. That was enough for her. She screamed, slid the latch open and tore out through the gate.

You can bet we four dogs were right behind her, out of that prison yard and into freedom. I slowed my pace to keep even with them. All three were yapping with excitement. I cautioned them to keep quiet because we were attracting too much attention. No good, they were just so happy they couldn't contain themselves.

Naturally a police car spotted us. The cop must have radioed for the local animal-control people because one of their vans arrived right away, and the attendants managed to scoop up all three of my companions.

Not me, of course. I wasn't about to let Jensen or Shawn or anybody else get their hands on me. I simply outran that animal-control crew without even looking back. Maybe they had had experience with Greyhounds before. They didn't even try to catch me.

Chapter Seven

I felt bad about the other three dogs. I can only hope the Shepherd and the Beagle got taken to an animal shelter and eventually found homes. No matter where they ended up, it was better than with the Jensens. I didn't worry about the little Bichon. She still had her tags on, so I'm sure she got back to her mistress.

But what was going to happen to me?

Believe it or not, my guardian angel, that wonderful Rescue Lady, came to my rescue again. She had taken the call from the principal at the school, and she began to worry when Janitor Jensen never arrived with me. Eventually she checked back with the school, and Jensen must have reported that I had run away. In any case, my angel got in her car and went looking for me. Not only that, she enlisted the aid of a whole army of volunteers in her rescue group, some of those great folks who had given shelter and foster care to Greyhounds like me. They kept scouring that whole area, and today I know enough to be thankful for their efforts.

One of the volunteers spotted me. Being big and black and skinny, I'm hard to miss. At first I didn't want to get caught, but then my Rescue Lady herself arrived. And I bounced up to her, tail wagging. Before you know it I was back in that familiar van and she was looking at me in that familiar way and shaking her head. "Stormy, Stormy, what am I going to do with you?"

Somehow she looked older now, more careworn, and I felt sorry for her. What if all the Greyhounds she had saved had given her as much trouble as I had? I licked her hand to show her I really was grateful.

As we drove, she continued, "I can't send you back to Amy. That boyfriend of hers, Shawn, the one you bit, would never allow it. And he's going to stay in the picture. Amy tells me she's going to marry the creep."

I felt stunned. It beats me how human beings, who are supposed to be smarter than us dogs, so often take a turn in their lives that they must know in their hearts is the worst thing for them. Why would a girl like Amy marry a man she knew would mistreat her and probably beat her? I'm only a dog, but I have better sense than that.

The Rescue Lady looked thoughtful. "There is a couple I think I can try you with," she said. "They have one Greyhound and they like her so well they want another. The dog they have is so shy, they think a companion will help her settle in."

Then the Rescue Lady stopped the car. She took my muzzle in both her hands and looked earnestly into my eyes. "Stormy, you have to understand something. This really is your last chance. My husband is retiring and we're moving to Florida. I won't be around to help you any more. You have to make this new home work for you."

Next day she drove me to a neat little house in a new development. A young couple, Sid and Dotty, greeted us at the door. Behind them I caught a glimpse of a small fawn-colored Greyhound.

Dotty introduced us to the dog. "This is Sheila," she announced. Then she turned around. "Oops, where did she go? She was here a minute ago."

"Sheila ran upstairs," Sid explained. "That's just like her. She doesn't like to meet anybody. She's scared of her own shadow."

I soon learned how true Sid's words were. Sheila was a beautiful dainty Greyhound about half my size. She had washed out at the track early on and was only two years old. She was lovely. I loved her from the start, but only like a sister, you understand. At first she would have nothing to do with me. She was afraid of everything, even me. She cowered and slunk away at the sight of anything strange. Dotty and Sid treated her with kindness, but she only learned to trust them slowly. Gradually she learned to like me.

Both our new owners worked, so we were left on our own most days. On weekends Dotty and Sid would take us on our leashes for walks in the country. Sometimes they would take us to visit their friends and even to Greyhound groups where we got to play with other dogs. Sheila was so shy she never enjoyed these trips and usually clung close to my side.

On the whole, life was pleasant. I had few complaints. As the Rescue Lady had told me, this was my last chance, and I wasn't about to mess it up. Sheila was good to be with, even though, just between us, at times she was a bit of a drag. Dotty and Sid gave us love, and I tried to love them back, as a good dog should.

Maybe, as I grew older, I was getting mellow. I didn't try to escape from the backyard even though I knew how. Sid had built a good tight fence, but it's amazing that people never seem to realize how easy gates are for a Greyhound to handle. This gate was as high as the fence, but it had plenty of handy wire spaces that I could get my paws into and so scramble over.

Well, I was a good boy, and I never did leap over except once until the last time. That first time was hardly my fault. I saw a gray cat ambling haughtily along just outside the yard. What's a Greyhound to do? I couldn't resist that. I hurtled over the gate, leaving little Sheila looking warily after me.

In a trice I was right behind that cat. She ducked into a yard across the street and scooted two houses down to dive through an open garage door.

I bounded behind her, then skidded to a stop. The cat stood guard over a basket, facing me with her back arched, claws extended, hissing like a steam kettle. Behind her in the basket I saw a gray mass of something moving. It was a bunch of kittens. Their frightened mewing joined their mother's angry hissing.

That's when I found out I was becoming an old softie. I couldn't go after that cat. Like a true Greyhound I had been bred and trained to chase moving things, and so I had done what I was supposed to do. But I just couldn't harm that mother and her little ones. I turned back to climb over the gate and rejoin Sheila. She licked my face, so I think she understood.

One day happiness seemed to burst forth in our little home. Sid let out the secret first. "It's true," he boomed. "I'm going to become a father!"

"Yes, my little doggies," Dotty told us, "we're going to have a baby. You'll have to learn to get along with a little brother or sister."

I don't think Sheila realized what this might mean for us, and I'm not sure I took it in fully myself. I only know that at that moment I felt a chill in the pit of my stomach. Dotty and Sid were happy, but I sensed trouble ahead.

It came two days later. I noticed that Dotty did not seem nearly as happy as when she first told us the news. Then I heard her talking on the phone, and that cold feeling stabbed my stomach even harder.

She was talking to the Greyhound rescue agency. "I'm sorry," she was saying. "My husband and I have decided it's just not possible to keep both dogs. Our house is small, and now with the baby coming . . ."

I listened aghast. She went on, "We love both the dogs. They would both be good with the baby, but the female, Sheila, is so shy I just don't know. The male, Stormy, is very friendly and outgoing, but he's big and he certainly has a mind of his own. My husband and I will have to think it over, and I'll let you know which of the two we'll have to let go."

My heart stood still. My fears had proved only too true. Our home was to be broken up.

I wish I could tell you all the things I thought of during the next day. First of all, I'm ashamed to say, I thought of myself. If I lost a home this time, no kindly Rescue Lady would be there to find me another. Sure, the other folks at the rescue agency would help, but they didn't have my lady's patience. And, let's face it, my record to date had been miserable. Would I ever find another home? And if I failed, what would become of me?

I wasn't entirely selfish. I thought of Sheila, too. Her plight was even worse than mine. She didn't have my hard-earned knowledge of the world. She didn't have my hard-won knack for getting out of tight spots. And she was so timid she might never get used to new owners. Out there, the cold world was even more cruel for her than it was for me.

That thought decided me. I knew what I had to do. I waited until the next morning for Dotty and Sid to leave for work. They would be gone about eight hours. These summer days they left Sheila and me in the backyard with plenty of water and shade. I didn't tell Sheila what I planned. I knew she would object. I just touched noses with her, then I scrambled over that fence for the last time.

I ran away, but slowly. I wanted to save my strength to put plenty of space between me and the house before Dotty and Sid got home. And this time I wanted to be sure none of the rescue volunteers could pick me up.

Where was I going? I had no plan. I just kept traveling, widening the distance between me and any pursuers. I was sure I had done the honorable thing. I was happy that I had fixed things so Sheila would be assured a home, but for me this was the low point of my life. I wondered if in all the world there could be a dog as homeless and friendless as I felt.

Chapter Eight

Eating up the miles, avoiding pedestrians, crossing the intersections with care, I had plenty of time to think. Looking back, I told myself that the reason I had never been able to find a real home was all my fault. I knew that the first job of any dog is to love and be loved. Had I failed? Yes, I told myself. Amy had given me a good home, but somehow I had never loved her with all my heart the way a good dog should. And Dotty and Sid, had I really given them my heart? I had to admit I had not.

In all these relationships I had held something back. I had failed to give all of myself. In my desolation I wondered why. What was

55

wrong with me? I didn't know it then, but I know the reason now. I had given my heart to somebody else.

All that miserable day, wandering I knew not where, I felt a complete failure. I had failed to keep a home. Worse, I had failed at loving. I didn't know where my next meal would come from, but that worry weighed far less upon me than the bitter thought that my whole life had been a failure.

And so I traveled. I have heard of animals who without realizing it retrace their steps back to the place of their birth or to a place where they had been happy. I don't know if I did this or not in those desperately unhappy hours. But it is a fact that, on purpose or not, my feet took me to the neighborhood of my first adopted home, where I had been truly happy so long ago.

It was mid-afternoon and it was hot. Kids were home from school on summer vacation. Often I had to avoid groups of them for fear of arousing attention. Down one side street I saw a group of boys racing each other pell-mell on their bikes. Now racing is something I know a bit about. I just couldn't resist joining in. Tired as I was, I took off after that pack of whirling wheels.

Down one street and up another those six boys pedaled madly. Then one kid took a turn too closely, slammed into the curb and crashed, bringing two others down with him. Two of the boys got up right away, but the third just lay there.

I got to him first. He was the smallest of the six. He lay crumpled up with his head down against the curb. I licked the side of his face and he turned over.

My heart stopped. The boy was my Davy.

Davy. Davy whom I had loved so much and had been forced to leave. I had found him. Or had I?

I think, even in that desperate moment when I thought he was badly hurt, when I feared I had found him only to lose him again, that everything came clear in my mind. It was Davy, though the poor lad never knew it, who had kept me from giving my heart to anyone else. It was because of Davy, because I had loved him so with all my doggy love, that I could never truly belong to anyone else.

Somebody must have called the ambulance because it came right away. They loaded Davy aboard and the big vehicle took off, lights flashing and siren blaring.

I ran then, ran as I had never run before. In the races of my early life I had put out every ounce of energy to beat the field. More recently I had managed some good speed to escape captors and get myself out of scrapes. But this was different. Now I ran as if my life depended on it. And it did.

You see, Davy was my life. I realized that now. I knew that nothing – nothing – was going to separate me from Davy again. I would follow that ambulance wherever it went. No matter that it flew faster than any other car or truck on the road. No matter that traffic all along the way screeched to a stop, that other vehicles pulled over to let it go by, that police officers waved it through stoplights. No matter that with every warning wail of the siren it picked up speed to fly down those suddenly emptied streets.

I am a Greyhound. If there is one thing I am created to do it is to run. This is bred into my blood and bone. Born to run. To run faster as the stakes grow higher. And now the stakes for me were the highest ever. I was running the race of my life.

I think the sight of the back end of that vehicle with the big letters AMBULANCE will burn into my brain until the day I die. I stretched every nerve to keep it in sight. It swerved around corners, tires screeching to match the siren. It picked up speed on the straight-aways, slowed to maneuver the curves, then speeded up again. Somehow I kept behind it. Twice I thought I had lost it. Three times cars almost hit me and I heard the horns blare. Once I heard a driver swear. But I dodged and ran harder.

My eyes stayed glued to the back of that vehicle. Now my breath came in great heaving gasps. My lungs felt on fire. My legs ached, my paw pads burned. But I ran. I ran as I had never run before. Other times I had run with all my strength. This time I ran with all my heart.

I think one more block might have finished me. But the ambulance slowed to turn at a sign that read "Emergency." In a moment it had stopped at the hospital entrance.

By the time I got there they had carried Davy on a stretcher into the building. I collapsed on a patch of grass near the emergency door, too exhausted to care if anyone noticed me.

We Greyhounds recover fast from even our fiercest runs, and in a few minutes I was able to drag myself to the shelter of a grove of trees. I was careful to keep the hospital door in view.

The next two hours were surely the longest of my life. Ambulances pulled up in a hurry, then pulled away. People moved in and out, in wheelchairs, on crutches and on their own feet. I knew there were other doors to that massive hospital, and I began to worry that I could miss Davy when he came out. Then I worried that he might be hurt so badly he could never get out, and that worry haunted me worst of all.

Nervously I ranged round and round that sprawling building. I don't know if you have ever noticed how many exits there are from a big hospital. It was confusing, and it proved scary, too. A truck marked "Security" kept circling around much as I was, and I had to keep clear.

I was getting desperate. Had I found my beloved Davy only to lose him again? Would he ever come out? Could he be dying back behind those cold brick walls?

I circled more and more frantically, throwing caution to the winds. Passersby noticed me now, and some even called or whistled. But I kept my distance. Nobody was going to keep me from my quest.

I think I must have given way to such nervous distraction and despair that I started whimpering to myself. I yearned for a sight of Davy as I had never yearned for anything in my life.

All of a sudden he was there. Down the steps of the front entrance he came, his mother and father on each side of him. He walked steadily, seeming no worse for wear, only a bandage around his head to show the injury.

Again my heart stopped. But my feet didn't. I needed but a single bound to leap up those hospital steps. Then I was on my hind legs, my tongue searching for Davy's face. He hugged and hugged me and he cried. I licked and licked. And I cried, too.

So I came home at last. Davy's father had found a new and better job and they had even bought a new house near their old one. They adopted me all over again, proper and legal.

Davy is older now and happier, and he has lots of friends. But he still has plenty of time for me. I've learned the blessing of a real place to call my own. And I've learned more. I know the gift of true love and I know the even greater gift of having a special someone to give my heart to.

Before I leave you, I'll let you in on a little secret: The backyard gate here is another easy one for any real racing Greyhound to jump over. But don't worry, I'm not going anywhere.

The End

About the Author

Boyd Wright, the author, is a retired newspaper editor who has written four books and numerous magazine articles. He lives in Mendham, N. J., with his wife, Jean, and their retired racing Greyhound, Jamie.

www.ingramcontent.com/pod-product-compliance
Lightning Source LLC
Chambersburg PA
CBHW020352290526
45785CB00005B/2243